MW00613304

Kindred Spirits

Promises for Mothers and Daughters

...inspired by life

Kindred Spirits: Promises for Mothers and Daughters
© 2008 Ellie Claire, Inc.
www.ellieclaire.com

Compiled by Barbara Farmer
Designed by Mick Thurber

ISBN 978-1-934770-09-2
Printed in China

Kindred Spirits

Promises for Mothers and Daughters

How It All Started

There is no other closeness in human life like the closeness between a mother and her baby—chronologically, physically, and spiritually they are just a few heartbeats away from being the same person.

SUSAN CHEVER

You made all the delicate, inner parts of my body
*   and knit me together in my mother's womb....*
You watched me as I was being formed in utter seclusion,
*   as I was woven together in the dark of the womb.*
You saw me before I was born.
*   Every day of my life was recorded in Your book.*
Every moment was laid out
*   before a single day had passed.*

PSALM 139:13, 15-16 NLT

Mothers of daughters are daughters of mothers and have remained so, in circles joined to circles, since time began.

SIGNE HAMMER

• • •

A daughter is one who reaches for your hand and touches your heart.

• • •

Everyday Is a Gift to Cherish

Everything in life is most fundamentally a gift. And you receive it best, and you live it best, by holding it with very open hands.

LEO O'DONOVAN

Go after a life of love as if your life depended on it—because it does. Give yourselves to the gifts God gives you. Most of all, try to proclaim His truth.

1 CORINTHIANS 14:1 THE MESSAGE

Time is a very precious gift of God; so precious that it's only given to us moment by moment.

AMELIA BARR

● ● ●

Every day we live is a priceless gift of God, loaded with possibilities to learn something new, to gain fresh insights.
DALE EVANS ROGERS

Close Connections

How many hopes and fears, how many ardent wishes and anxious apprehensions are twisted together in the threads that connect the parent with the child!

SAMUEL GRISWOLD GOODRICH

The healthiest relationships are those that "breathe"—that is, they move out from one another for a few days and then come back together for a time of closeness.

JAMES DOBSON

Let us hold tightly without wavering to the hope we affirm, for God can be trusted to keep His promise. Let us think of ways to motivate one another to acts of love and good works. And let us not neglect our meeting together, as some people do, but encourage one another.

HEBREWS 10:23-25 NLT

• • •

I am yours, you are mine.
Of this we are certain.
You are lodged in my heart, the small key is lost.
You must stay there forever.
FRAU AVA

• • •

A Fountain of Gladness

When we do the best that we can, we never know what miracle is wrought in our life, or in the life of another.

HELEN KELLER

The wise are known for their understanding. Their pleasant words make them better teachers. Understanding is like a fountain which gives life to those who use it.

PROVERBS 16:21-22 NCV

Kindness has been described in many ways. It is the poetry of the heart, the music of the world. It is the golden chain which binds society together. It is a fountain of gladness.

THE WAR CRY

● ● ●

*A kind heart is a fountain of gladness, making everything
in its vicinity freshen into smiles.*
WASHINGTON IRVING

Living Together

Mother had a thousand thoughts to get through within a day, and...most of these were about avoiding disaster.

NATALIE KUSZ

A family is a unit composed not only of children but of men, women, an occasional animal, and the common cold.

OGDEN NASH

You're blessed when you can show people how to cooperate instead of compete or fight. That's when you discover who you really are, and your place in God's family.

MATTHEW 5:9 THE MESSAGE

Each day of our lives we make deposits in the memory banks of our children.

CHARLES R. SWINDOLL

• • •

*Family life is too intimate to be preserved by the spirit of justice.
It can be sustained by a spirit of love which goes beyond justice.*
REINHOLD NIEBUHR

Blessings Await

Having someone who understands is a great blessing for ourselves. Being someone who understands is a great blessing to others.

JANETTE OKE

Lift up your eyes. Your heavenly Father waits to bless you—in inconceivable ways to make your life what you never dreamed it could be.

ANNE ORTLUND

God can pour on the blessings in astonishing ways so that you're ready for anything and everything, more than just ready to do what needs to be done.

2 CORINTHIANS 9:8 THE MESSAGE

• • •

*Some blessings—like rainbows after rain or a friend's listening ear—
are extraordinary gifts waiting to be discovered in an ordinary day.*

• • •

God's Gift to Each Other

Among God's best gifts to us are the people who love us.

But what happens when we live God's way? He brings gifts into our lives, much the same way that fruit appears in an orchard—things like affection for others, exuberance about life, serenity. We develop a willingness to stick with things, a sense of compassion in the heart, and a conviction that a basic holiness permeates things and people. We find ourselves involved in loyal commitments, not needing to force our way in life, able to marshal and direct our energies wisely.

GALATIANS 5:22-23 THE MESSAGE

Not what we give, but what we share,
For the gift without the giver is bare.

JAMES RUSSELL LOWELL

Every one has a gift for something, even if it is the gift of being a good friend.

MARIAN ANDERSON

● ● ●

Having someone who understands is a great blessing for ourselves.
Being someone who understands is a great blessing to others.
JANETTE OKE

● ● ●

A Countenance Is Made Beautiful

Joy is the echo of God's life within us.

JOSEPH MARMION

God has made everything beautiful for its own time. He has planted eternity in the human heart.

ECCLESIASTES 3:11 NLT

Into all our lives, in simple, familiar, homely ways, God infuses this element of joy from the surprises of life, which unexpectedly brighten our days and fill our eyes with light.

HENRY WADSWORTH LONGFELLOW

Think of all the beauty still left around you and be happy.

ANNE FRANK

•••

As a countenance is made beautiful by the soul's shining through it,
so the world is beautiful by the shining through it of God.
FRIEDRICH HEINRICH JACOBI

Treasure Today

In ordinary life we hardly realize that we receive a great deal more than we give, and that it is only with gratitude that life becomes rich.

DIETRICH BONHOEFFER

For the Lord grants wisdom!
From His mouth come knowledge and understanding.
He grants a treasure of common sense to the honest.
He is a shield to those who walk with integrity.
He guards the paths of the just
and protects those who are faithful to Him.
Then you will understand what is right, just, and fair,
and you will find the right way to go.

PROVERBS 2:5-9 NLT

Normal day, let me be aware of the treasure you are. Let me learn from you, love you, bless you before you depart. Let me not pass you by in quest of some rare and perfect tomorrow.

• • •

See each morning a world made anew, as if it were the morning of the very first day;...treasure and use it, as if it were the final hour of the very last day.
FAY HARTZELL ARNOLD

• • •

A Special Place in My Heart

A son is a son till he takes him a wife, a daughter is a daughter all of her life.

IRISH SAYING

Youth fades; love droops, the leaves of friendship fall;
A mother's secret hope outlives them all.

OLIVER WENDELL HOLMES

Love one another deeply, from the heart.

1 PETER 1:22 NIV

A mother understands what a child does not say.

JEWISH PROVERB

Being with you is like walking on a very clear morning—
definitely the sensation of belonging there.

E. B. WHITE

• • •

Your life is a gift from God,
And it is a privilege to share it.
Today and always,
Know that you have a very special place in my heart—
And in His.

● ● ●

Simple and Natural Things

The splendor of the rose and the whiteness of the lily do not rob the little violet of its scent nor the daisy of its simple charm. If every tiny flower wanted to be a rose, spring would lose its loveliness.

THÉRÈSE OF LISIEUX

> *I'm asking God for one thing,*
> *only one thing:*
> *To live with Him in His house*
> *my whole life long.*
> *I'll contemplate His beauty;*
> *I'll study at His feet.*
> *That's the only quiet, secure place*
> *in a noisy world.*

PSALM 27:4-5 THE MESSAGE

Happy people...enjoy the fundamental, often very simple things of life.... They savor the moment, glad to be alive, enjoying their work, their families, the good things around them. They are adaptable; they can bend with the wind, adjust to the changes in their times, enjoy the contest of life.... Their eyes are turned outward; they are aware, compassionate. They have the capacity to love.

JANE CANFIELD

From the simple seeds of understanding, we reap the lovely harvest of true friendship.

Our Story

Like branches on a tree, we grow in different directions, yet our roots remain as one. Each of our lives will always be a special part of the other.

Sisters, we taught you how to live in a way that will please God, and you are living that way. Now we ask and encourage you in the Lord Jesus to live that way even more.

1 Thessalonians 4:1 NCV

Soft as some song divine, thy story flows.

Homer

The Story of your life will be the story of prayer and answers to prayer.

Ole Hallesby

• • •

*Our true places as women in God's Story are as diverse
and unique as wildflowers in a field.*
JOHN AND STASI ELDREDGE

● ● ●

A Feeling that Nurtures the Soul

Can you see the holiness in those things you take for granted—a paved road or a washing machine? If you concentrate on finding what is good in every situation, you will discover that your life will suddenly be filled with gratitude, a feeling that nurtures the soul.

HAROLD KUSHNER

It is good to give thanks to the Lord
  And to sing praises to Your name, O Most High;
To declare Your lovingkindness in the morning
  And Your faithfulness by night,

PSALM 92:1-2 NASB

Gratitude. More aware of what you have than what you don't. Recognizing the treasure in the simple—a child's hug, fertile soil, a golden sunset. Relishing in the comfort of the common—a warm bed, a hot meal, a clean shirt.

MAX LUCADO

● ● ●

Gratitude is not only the greatest of virtues, but the parent of all others.
Cicero

Mother Love

A Mother's love is something
   that no on can explain,
It is made of deep devotion
   and of sacrifice and pain....
It believes beyond believing
   when the world around condemns,
And it glows with all the beauty
   of the rarest, brightest gems.

HELEN STEINER RICE

As high as heaven is over the earth,
   so strong is His love to those who fear Him....
As parents feel for their children,
   God feels for those who fear Him.

PSALM 103:11, 13 THE MESSAGE

A mother is not a person to lean on, but a person to make
leaning unnecessary.

DOROTHY CANFIELD FISHER

There is an enduring tenderness in the love of a mother...
that transcends all other affections of the heart.
WASHINGTON IRVING

Share the Secret

To be able to find joy in another's joy, that is
the secret of happiness.

Know that I'm on your side, right alongside you. You're not in
this alone. I want you woven into a tapestry of love, in touch
with everything there is to know of God. Then you will have
minds confident and at rest, focused on Christ, God's great
mystery. All the richest treasures of wisdom and knowledge are
embedded in that mystery and nowhere else.

Colossians 2:1-2 the message

The secret of life is that all we have and are
is a gift of grace to be shared.

Lloyd John Ogilvie

One single grateful thought raised to heaven is the
most perfect prayer.

G. E. Lessing

*The real secret of happiness is not what you give
or what you receive, it's what you share.*

Daughter of Mine

My beautiful daughter, love of my heart,
    I hope that you know you're wonderful and smart.
I cherish you dearly for the person you are;
    You have passion and caring that will carry you far....
You have my love forever;
    I adored you from the start;
It's a privilege to be your mother,
    Dear daughter of my heart.

CARI VICK

Facing a mirror you see merely your own countenance; facing your
child you finally understand how everyone else has seen you.

DANIEL RAEBURN

Many daughters have done well,
    But you excel them all.

PROVERBS 31:29 NKJV

A little girl is...innocence playing in the mud, beauty standing
on its head, and motherhood dragging a doll by the foot.

ALAN BECK

● ● ●

My daughter is joy personified to me.
JANIE HARPER FORD

● ● ●

How High Our Dreams Can Soar

God's gifts put man's best dreams to shame.

ELIZABETH BARRETT BROWNING

Allow your dreams a place in your prayers and plans. God-given dreams can help you move into the future He is preparing for you.

BARBARA JOHNSON

More things are wrought by prayer
  Than this world dreams of.

ALFRED, LORD TENNYSON

God can do anything, you know—far more than you could ever imagine or guess or request in your wildest dreams! He does it...by working within us, His Spirit deeply and gently within us.

EPHESIANS 3:20 THE MESSAGE

• • •

The stars exist that we might know how high our dreams can soar.

⸻

God Knows You

God not only knows us, but He values us highly in spite of all
He knows.... You and I are the creatures He prizes above the rest
of His creation. We are made in His image and He sacrificed
His Son that each one of us might be one with Him.

JOHN FISHER

O Lord, You have examined my heart
    and know everything about me.
You know when I sit down or stand up.
    You know my thoughts even when I'm far away.
You see me when I travel
    and when I rest at home.
You know everything I do.
    You know what I am going to say....
You go before me and follow me.
    You place Your hand of blessing on my head.

PSALM 139:1-5 NLT

God knows everything about us. And He cares about everything.
Moreover, He can manage every situation. And He loves us!
Surely this is enough to open the wellsprings of joy.... And joy is
always a source of strength.

HANNAH WHITALL SMITH

● ● ●

God created the universe, but He also created you. God knows you,
God loves you, and God cares about the tiniest details of your life.
BRUCE BICKEL AND STAN JANTZ

Trusting God

A mother who walks with God knows He only asks her to take care of the possible and to trust Him with the impossible.

RUTH BELL GRAHAM

Trust in the Lord with all your heart,
And lean not on your own understanding;
In all your ways acknowledge Him,
And He shall direct your paths.

PROVERBS 3:5-6 NKJV

God loves and cares for us, even to the least event and smallest need of life.

HENRY EDWARD MANNING

● ● ●

God still draws near to us in the ordinary, commonplace, everyday experiences and places.... He comes in surprising ways.
HENRY GARIEPY

Love Wrapped Up for You

But me He caught—reached all the way
    from sky to sea; He pulled me out
Of that ocean of hate, that enemy chaos,
    the void in which I was drowning.
They hit me when I was down,
    but God stuck by me.
He stood me up on a wide-open field;
    I stood there saved—surprised to be loved!

PSALM 18:18-19 THE MESSAGE

To receive a gift, molded from love and sacrifice, selected with
care and tied up with all the excitement the giver has to offer, is
indeed rare. They don't come along often, but when they do,
cherish them.

ERMA BOMBECK

I wished I had a box, the biggest I could find,
    I'd fill it right up to the brim with everything that's kind.
A box without a lock, of course, and never any key;
    for everything inside that box would then be offered free.
Grateful words for joys received I'd freely give away.
    Oh, let us open wide a box of praise for every day.

● ● ●

*Each day is a treasure box of gifts from God, just waiting to be opened.
Open your gifts with excitement. You will find forgiveness attached to ribbons
of joy. You will find love wrapped in sparkling gems.*
JOAN CLAYTON

Family Ties

There's no vocabulary
    For love within a family, love that's lived in
But not looked at, love within the light of which
    All else is seen, the love within which
All other love finds speech.

T. S. ELIOT

Happiness is being at peace, being with loved ones, being comfortable... But most of all, it's having those loved ones.

JOHNNY CASH

As for me and my family, we will serve the Lord.

JOSHUA 24:15 NLT

When you look at your life, the greatest happinesses are family happinesses.

JOYCE BROTHERS

I know of no realm of life that can provide more companionship in a lonely world or greater feelings of security and purpose in chaotic times than the close ties of a family.
CHARLES R. SWINDOLL

• • •

Truly You

Everybody can be great. Because anybody can serve. You don't have to have a college degree to serve. You don't have to make your subject and your verb agree to serve.... You only need a heart full of grace. A soul generated by love.

MARTIN LUTHER KING JR.

Greatness lies not in being strong, but in the right use of strength.

HENRY WARD BEECHER

I pray that from His glorious, unlimited resources He will empower you with inner strength through His Spirit. Then Christ will make His home in your hearts as you trust in Him. Your roots will grow down into God's love and keep you strong.

EPHESIANS 3:16-17 NLT

What is strength without a double share of wisdom?

JOHN MILTON

What lies behind us and what lies before us are tiny matters compared to what lies within us.
RALPH WALDO EMERSON

Forgiveness Is the Answer

The heart of a mother is a deep abyss at the bottom of which you will always find forgiveness.

HONORE DE BALZAC

Live creatively, friends. If someone falls into sin, forgivingly restore him, saving your critical comments for yourself. You might be needing forgiveness before the day's out. Stoop down and reach out to those who are oppressed. Share their burdens, and so complete Christ's law.

GALATIANS 6:1-3 THE MESSAGE

Love has been called the most effective motivational force in all the world. When love is at work in us, it is remarkable how giving and forgiving, understanding and tolerant we can be.

CHARLES R. SWINDOLL

• • •

Forgiveness is the answer to the child's dream of a miracle by which what is broken is made whole again, what is soiled is again made clean.
DAG HAMMARSKJOLD

The Attention of God

We have been in God's thought from all eternity, and in His creative love, His attention never leaves us.

MICHAEL QUOIST

May you have the power to understand, as all God's people should, how wide, how long, how high, and how deep His love is.

EPHESIANS 3:18 NLT

If you have a special need today, focus your full attention on the goodness and greatness of your Father rather than on the size of your need. Your need is so small compared to His ability to meet it.

● ● ●

God is every moment totally aware of each one of us. Totally aware in intense concentration and love.... No one passes through any area of life, happy or tragic, without the attention of God.

EUGENIA PRICE

Homemade Things

So many things we love are you, I can't seem to explain except
by little things, but flowers and beautiful handmade things—
small stitches. So much of our reading and thinking, so many
sweet customs and so much of our...well, religion. It is all you.

ANNE MORROW LINDBERGH

These commandments that I give you today are to be upon
your hearts. Impress them on your children. Talk about them
when you sit at home and when you walk along the road,
when you lie down and when you get up.

DEUTERONOMY 6:6-7 NIV

Prayers arising out of the context of the family are perhaps
the most common expression of praying.... As we pray in the
context of the family, we learn that holiness is homemade.

RICHARD J. FOSTER

● ● ●

The most important things in your home are people.
BARBARA JOHNSON

What Is Essential

You're blessed when you get your inside world—your mind and heart—put right. Then you can see God in the outside world.

MATTHEW 5:8 THE MESSAGE

Nothing is so strong as gentleness, and nothing so gentle as real strength.

FRANCIS DE SALES

Pursue righteousness, godliness, faith, love, endurance and gentleness. Fight the good fight of the faith. Take hold of the eternal life to which you were called when you made your good confession in the presence of many witnesses.

1 TIMOTHY 6:11-12 NIV

• • •

The human contribution is the essential ingredient. It is only in the giving of oneself to others that we truly live.
ETHEL PERCY ANDRUS

A Smile Costs Nothing

A smile is a curve that sets everything straight.

PHYLLIS DILLER

A smile is a light in the window of the soul indicating that the heart is at home.

The thing that goest farthest towards making life worth while,
That costs the least, and does the most, is just a pleasant smile....
It's full of worth and goodness too, with manly kindness blent,
It's worth a million dollars and it doesn't cost a cent.

WILBUR D. NESBIT

A happy heart makes the face cheerful.

PROVERBS 15:13 NIV

• • •

*A smile costs nothing but gives much. It takes but a moment,
and the memory of it sometimes lasts forever.*

The Friend I've Found in You

Few delights can equal the mere presence of one whom we trust utterly.

GEORGE MACDONALD

My best friend
my mom
Both in one
God truly did give you the gift
of a mother's love

GRACE HAYS

This is My commandment, that you love one other, just as I have loved you. Greater love has no one than this, that one lay down his life for his friends.

JOHN 15:12-13 NASB

I breathed a song into the air,
It fell to earth, I know not where...
and the song, from beginning to end,
I found again in the heart of a friend.

HENRY WADSWORTH LONGFELLOW

● ● ●

Insomuch as any one pushes you nearer to God, he or she is your friend.
FRENCH PROVERB

Attitude Is Everything

If you have any encouragement from being united with Christ, if any comfort from His love, if any fellowship with the Spirit, if any tenderness and compassion, then make my joy complete by being like-minded, having the same love, being one in spirit and purpose. Do nothing out of selfish ambition or vain conceit, but in humility consider others better than yourselves.

PHILIPPIANS 2:1-3 NIV

'Tis easy enough to be pleasant,
When life flows along like a song;
But the man worthwhile is the one who will smile
When everything does dead wrong;
For the test of the heart is trouble,
And it always comes with the years,
But the smile that is worth the praise of earth
Is the smile that comes through tears.

ELLA WHEELER WILCOX

A positive attitude may not solve all your problems, but it will annoy enough people to make it worth the effort.

HERM ALBRIGHT

● ● ●

A strong positive mental attitude will create more miracles than any wonder drug.
PATRICIA NEAL

A Daughter Is...

...a little girl who grows up to be a friend.

...the happy memories of the past, the joyful moments of the present, and the hope and promise of the future.

...a day brightener and a heart warmer.

...a mother's gender partner, her closest ally in the family confederacy, an extension of her self.

...a mother's treasure.

May our daughters be like graceful pillars,
carved to beautify a palace.
PSALM 144:12 NLT

Love Isn't Love 'til You Give It Away

You're here to be light, bringing out the God-colors in the world. God is not a secret to be kept. We're going public with this, as public as a city on a hill. If I make you light-bearers, you don't think I'm going to hide you under a bucket, do you? I'm putting you on a light stand. Now that I've put you there on a hilltop, on a light stand—shine! Keep open house; be generous with your lives. By opening up to others, you'll prompt people to open up with God, this generous Father in heaven.

MATTHEW 5:14 THE MESSAGE

The true meaning of life is to plant trees, under whose shade you do not expect to sit.

NELSON HENDERSON

Love in the heart wasn't put there to stay;
Love isn't love 'til you give it away.
OSCAR HAMMERSTEIN II

Not So Little Anymore

You know children are growing up when they start asking questions that have answers.

J. J. PLOMP

My child, never forget the things I have taught you.
Store my commands in your heart.
If you do this, you will live many years,
and your life will be satisfying.

PROVERBS 3:1-2 NLT

Open her eyes to the blessings around her;
Show her that beauty and goodness surround her.
Help her to trust in the future, not fear it;
Teach her that dreams are the winds of the Spirit.
Guide her with wisdom and gentle persuasion;
For she is God's pleasure—His flower of creation.

Watching your daughter being collected by her date feels like
handing over a million dollar Stradivarius to a gorilla.

JIM BISHOP

● ● ●

A daughter may outgrow your lap, but she will never outgrow your heart.

Body and Spirit

I think that anyone who comes upon a Nautilus machine suddenly will agree with me that its prototype was clearly invented at some time in history when torture was considered a reasonable alternative to diplomacy.

Anna Quindlen

Dig where the gold is...unless you just need some exercise.

John M. Capozzi

Don't depend on your own wisdom. Respect the Lord and refuse to do wrong. Then your body will be healthy, and your bones will be strong. Honor the Lord with your wealth and the firstfruits from all your crops. Then your barns will be full, and your wine barrels will overflow with new wine.

Proverbs 3:7-10 ncv

• • •

I believe that every human has a finite number of heart-beats.
I don't intend to waste any of mine running around doing exercises.
BUZZ ALDRIN

My Prayer for You

I love you so, my daughter,
And I never cease to pray
that God will guard and keep you safe
within His love each day.
May you be guided by His word
In all you say and do,
For all the pride of life for me
Is centered, dear daughter, in you.

JANIE HARPER FORD

We always thank God for all of you and pray for you
constantly. As we pray to our God and Father about you,
we think of your faithful work, your loving deeds, and the
enduring hope you have because of our Lord Jesus Christ.

1 THESSALONIANS 1:2-3 NLT

• • •

I said a prayer for you today
And I know God must have heard;
I felt the answer in my heart
Although He spoke no word...
I asked for happiness for you
In all things great and small,
But it was His loving care
I prayed for most of all.

_____

_____

_____

_____

_____

_____

_____

_____

_____

_____

_____

● ● ●

The Art of Courage

Courage is doing what you're afraid to do. There can be no courage unless you're scared.

EDDIE RICKENBACKER

Courage is the art of being the only one who knows you're scared to death.

HAROLD WILSON

This is my command—be strong and courageous! Do not be afraid or discouraged. For the Lord your God is with you wherever you go.

JOSHUA 1:9 NLT

I wanted you to see what real courage is.... It's when you know you're licked before you begin but you begin anyway and you see it through no matter what.

HARPER LEE

The only courage that matters is the kind that gets you from one moment to the next.

MIGNON MCLAUGHLIN

Courage is fear that has said its prayers.
DOROTHY BERNARD

Simple Tastes, Inside and Out

We are indeed much more than what we eat, but what we eat can nevertheless help us to be much more than what we are.

ADELLE DAVIS

I base my fashion taste on what doesn't itch.

GILDA RADNER

Food is an important part of a balanced diet.

FRAN LEBOWITZ

Don't fuss about what's on the table at mealtimes or if the clothes in your closet are in fashion. There is far more to your inner life than the food you put in your stomach, more to your outer appearance than the clothes you hang on your body. Look at the ravens, free and unfettered, not tied down to a job description, carefree in the care of God. And you count far more.

LUKE 12:22-24 THE MESSAGE

• • •

Fashion is something that goes in one year and out the other.

Only One Mother in the World

The most important thing she'd learned over the years was that there was no way to be a perfect mother and a million ways to be a good one.

JILL CHURCHILL

God made a wonderful mother,
A mother who never grows old;
He made her smile of the sunshine,
And He molded her heart of pure gold;
In her eyes He placed bright shining stars,
In her cheeks, fair roses you see;
God made a wonderful mother,
And He gave that dear mother to me.

PAT O'REILLY

We cared for you the way a mother cares for her children.
We loved you dearly.

1 THESSALONIANS 2:6 THE MESSAGE

• • •

Most of all the other beautiful things in life come by twos and threes, by dozens and hundreds. Plenty of roses, stars, sunsets, rainbows, brothers and sisters, aunts and cousins, comrades and friends—but only one mother in the whole world.
KATE DOUGLAS WIGGIN

The Generous Spirit

You must give some time to your fellow men. Even if it's a little thing, do something for others—something for which you get no pay but the privilege of doing it.

ALBERT SCHWEITZER

When you give a lunch or a dinner, don't invite only your friends, your family, your other relatives, and your rich neighbors. At another time they will invite you to eat with them, and you will be repaid. Instead, when you give a feast, invite the poor, the crippled, the lame, and the blind. Then you will be blessed, because they have nothing and cannot pay you back.
Luke 14:12-14 ncv

Make all you can, save all you can, give all you can.

JOHN WESLEY

We make a living by what we get, we make a life by what we give.

SIR WINSTON CHURCHILL

Give what you have. To someone, it may be better than you dare to think.
HENRY WADSWORTH LONGFELLOW

Life, Love, and Laughter

Sometimes the laughter in mothering is the recognition of the ironies and absurdities. Sometime, though, it's just pure, unthinking delight.

BARBARA SCHAPIRO

She is clothed with strength and dignity; she can laugh at the days to come.

PROVERBS 31:25 NIV

Families give us many things—love and meaning, purpose and an opportunity to give, and a sense of humor.

The real joy of life is in its play. Play is anything we do for the joy and love of doing it, apart from any profit, compulsion, or sense of duty. It is the real living of life.

WALTER RAUSCHENBUSCH

• • •

A good laugh is sunshine in a house.

Slow Down and Enjoy Life

Many persons have a wrong idea of what constitutes true happiness. It is not attained through self-gratification but through fidelity to a worthy purpose.

HELEN KELLER

Dear friend, I pray that you may enjoy good health and that all may go well with you, even as your soul is getting along well.

3 JOHN 1:2 NIV

Most folks are about as happy as they make up their minds to be.

ABRAHAM LINCOLN

● ● ●

Slow down and enjoy life. It's not only the scenery you miss by going too fast—
you also miss the sense of where you are going and why.

EDDIE CANTOR

Truest Friends

A mother is the truest friend we have, when trials, heavy and sudden, fall upon us; when adversity takes the place of prosperity; when friends who rejoice with us in our sunshine, desert us when troubles thicken around us, still will she cling to us, and endeavor by her kind precepts and counsels to dissipate the clouds of darkness, and cause peace to return to our hearts.

WASHINGTON IRVING

Life is to be fortified by many friendships. To love and to be loved is the greatest happiness of existence.

WALTER WINCHELL

Perfume and incense bring joy to the heart, and the pleasantness of one's friend springs from his earnest counsel.

PROVERBS 27:9 NIV

Then come the wild weather,
come sleet or come snow,
we will stand by each other,
however it blow.
SIMON DACH

Kaleidoscope of New Possibilities

To see a world in a grain of sand,
And a heaven in a wild flower,
Hold infinity in the palm of your hand,
And eternity in an hour.

WILLIAM BLAKE

You see things as they are and ask, "Why?" I dream things
as they never were and ask, "Why not?"

GEORGE BERNARD SHAW

Happy are those who hear the joyful call to worship,
for they will walk in the light of Your presence, Lord.
They rejoice all day long in Your wonderful reputation.
They exult in Your righteousness.
You are their glorious strength.
It pleases You to make us strong.

PSALM 89:15-17 NLT

• • •

Remember that happiness is a way of travel—not a destination.
Roy M. Goodman

Inside and Out

Don't be concerned about the outward beauty of fancy hairstyles, expensive jewelry, or beautiful clothes. You should clothe yourselves instead with the beauty that comes from within, the unfading beauty of a gentle and quiet spirit, which is so precious to God.

1 PETER 3:3-4 NLT

In every man's heart there is a secret nerve that answers to the vibrations of beauty.

CHRISTOPHER MORLEY

A woman of beauty...knows in her quiet center where God dwells that He finds her beautiful, and deemed her worthy, and in Him, she is enough.

JOHN AND STASI ELDREDGE

You can take no credit for beauty at sixteen. But if you are beautiful at sixty, it will be your soul's own doing.
MARIE CARMICHAEL STOPES

Hope for Today

Hope begins in the dark, the stubborn hope that if you just show up and try to do the right thing, the dawn will come. You wait and watch and work: You don't give up.

ANNE LAMOTT

This I call to mind and therefore I have hope: Because of the Lord's great love we are not consumed, for His compassions never fail. They are new every morning; great is Your faithfulness.

LAMENTATIONS 3:21-23 NCV

Do not spoil what you have by desiring what you have not; but remember that what you now have was once among the things you only hoped for.

EPICURUS

It is difficult to say what is impossible, for the dream of yesterday is the hope of today and the reality of tomorrow.
ROBERT H. GODDARD

● ● ●

Real Joy

I've grown to realize the joy that comes from little victories is preferable to the fun that comes from ease and the pursuit of pleasure.

LAWANA BLACKWELL

May the God of hope fill you with all joy and peace as you trust in Him, so that you may overflow with hope.

ROMANS 15:13 NIV

Real joy comes not from ease or riches or from the praise of men, but from doing something worthwhile.

SIR WILFRED GRENFELL

Joyful are people of integrity,
who follow the instructions of the Lord.
Joyful are those who obey His laws
and search for Him with all their hearts.

PSALM 119:1-2 NLT

There is no greater joy nor greater reward than to make a fundamental difference in someone's life.
MARY ROSE McGEADY

• • •

Dreaming Dreams

If you have built castles in the air, your work need not be lost; that is where they should be. Now put the foundations under them.

HENRY DAVID THOREAU

We constantly pray for you, that our God may count you worthy of His calling, and that by His power He may fulfill every good purpose of yours and every act prompted by your faith.

2 THESSALONIANS 1:11 NIV

This is part of the essence of motherhood, watching your kid grow into her own person and not being able to do anything about it. Otherwise children would be nothing more than pets.

HEATHER ARMSTRONG

At every crossroad, follow your dream. It is courageous to let your heart lead the way.
THOMAS LELAND

_____

_____

_____

_____

_____

_____

_____

● ● ●

Making a Difference

Character is like a tree and reputation like its shadow. The shadow is what we think of it; the tree is the real thing.

ABRAHAM LINCOLN

People grow through experience if they meet life honestly and courageously. This is how character is built.

ELEANOR ROOSEVELT

We can rejoice, too, when we run into problems and trials, for we know that they help us develop endurance. And endurance develops strength of character, and character strengthens our confident hope of salvation. And this hope will not lead to disappointment. For we know how dearly God loves us, because He has given us the Holy Spirit to fill our hearts with His love.

ROMANS 5:3-5 NLT

Character cannot be developed in ease and quiet. Only through experience of trial and suffering can the soul be strengthened, ambition inspired, and success achieved.

HELEN KELLER

Personality can open doors, but only character can keep them open.
ELMER G. LETTERMAN

One Big Happy Family

Family faces are magic mirrors. Looking at people who belong to us, we see the past, present, and future.

GAIL LUMET BUCKLEY

Let us not become weary in doing good, for at the proper time we will reap a harvest if we do not give up. Therefore, as we have opportunity, let us do good to all people, especially to those who belong to the family of believers.

GALATIANS 6:9-10 NIV

What families have in common the world around is that they are the place where people learn who they are and how to be that way.

JEAN ILLSLEY CLARKE

• • •

Call it clan, call it a network, call it a tribe, call it a family.
Whatever you call it, whoever you are, you need one.
JANE HOWARD

The Treasure of Kindness

I expect to pass through this world but once; any good thing
therefore that I can do, or any kindness that I can show to any
fellow creature, let me do it now; let me not defer or neglect it,
for I shall not pass this way again.

STEPHEN GRELLET

Never let loyalty and kindness leave you!...
Write them deep within your heart.
Then you will find favor with both God and people,
and you will earn a good reputation.

PROVERBS 3:3-4 NLT

Kindness is the only service that will stand the storm of life and
not wash out. It will wear well and be remembered long after
the prism of politeness or the complexion of courtesy has faded
away. When I am gone, I hope it can be said of me that I
plucked a thistle and planted a flower wherever I thought a
flower would grow.

• • •

The ideals which have lighted my way, and time after time have given me new courage to face life cheerfully, have been Kindness, Beauty, and Truth.
ALBERT EINSTEIN

Spending Time

Besides the noble art of getting things done, there is a nobler art of leaving things undone. The wisdom of life consists in the elimination of nonessentials.

LIN YUTANG

An unhurried sense of time is in itself a form of wealth.

BONNIE FRIEDMAN

To everything there is a season,
A time for every purpose under heaven.

ECCLESIASTES 3:1 NKJV

Time is the coin of your life. It is the only coin you have, and only you can determine how it will be spent. Be careful lest you let other people spend it for you.

CARL SANDBURG

• • •

This time, like all times, is a very good one, if we but know what to do with it.
RALPH WALDO EMERSON

Home Sweet Home

Into all our lives, in simple, familiar, homely ways, God infuses this element of joy from the surprises of life, which unexpectedly brighten our days and fill our eyes with light.

HENRY WADSWORTH LONGFELLOW

In the presence of the Lord your God, you and your families...shall rejoice in everything you have put your hand to, because the Lord your God has blessed you.

DEUTERONOMY 12:7 NIV

Make two homes for thyself, my daughter. One actual home...and another spiritual home, which thou art to carry with thee always.

CATHERINE OF SIENNA

• • •

Where we love is home, home that our feet may leave, but not our hearts.
OLIVER WENDELL HOLMES

Natural Wonders

If we are cheerful and contented, all nature smiles...the flowers are more fragrant, the birds sing more sweetly, and the sun, moon, and stars all appear more beautiful and seem to rejoice with us.

ORISON SWETT MARDEN

What a wildly wonderful world, God! You made it all, with Wisdom at Your side, made earth overflow with Your wonderful creations.... All the creatures look expectantly to You to give them their meals on time. You come, and they gather around; You open Your hand and they eat from it.... Take back Your Spirit and they die, revert to original mud; Send out Your Spirit and they spring to life.

PSALM 104:24-30 THE MESSAGE

Just as a prism of glass miters light and casts a colored braid, a garden sings sweet incantations the human heart strains to hear. Hiding in every flower, in every leaf, in every twig and bough, are reflections of the God who once walked with us in Eden.

TONIA TRIEBWASSER

• • •

Beauty puts a face on God. When we gaze at nature, at a loved one, at a work of art, our soul immediately recognizes and is drawn to the face of God.
MARGARET BROWNLEY

Sunshine and Smiles

What sunshine is to flowers, smiles are to humanity. These are but trifles, to be sure; but, scattered along life's pathway, the good they do is inconceivable.

JOSEPH ADDISON

One day spent in Your house, this beautiful place of worship, beats thousands spent on Greek island beaches.... All sunshine and sovereign is God, generous in gifts and glory.

PSALM 84:10-11 THE MESSAGE

I am still determined to be cheerful and happy, in whatever situation I may be; for I have also learned from experience that the greater part of our happiness or misery depends upon our dispositions, and not upon our circumstances.

MARTHA WASHINGTON

● ● ●

Nothing's better than the wind to your back, the sun in front of you, and your friends beside you.
AARON DOUGLAS TRIMBLE

Wonder-filled Times

If a child is to keep his inborn sense of wonder...he needs the companionship of at least one adult who can share it, rediscovering with him the joy, excitement, and mystery of the world we live in.

RACHEL CARSON

I call on You, O God, for You will answer me;
give ear to me and hear my prayer.
Show the wonder of Your great love,
You who save by Your right hand
those who take refuge in You from their foes.
Keep me as the apple of Your eye;
hide me in the shadow of Your wings.

PSALM 17:6-8 NIV

• • •

Life is what we are alive to. It is not length but breadth.... Be alive to...goodness, kind-ness, purity, love, history, poetry, music, flowers, stars, God, and eternal hope.
MALTBIE D. BABCOCK

The Grand Essentials

Prayer is essential.... Pray hard and long. Pray for your brothers and sisters. Keep your eyes open. Keep each other's spirits up so that no one falls behind.

EPHESIANS 6:13 THE MESSAGE

This is the true joy of life, the being used up for a purpose recognized by yourself as a mighty one; being a force of nature instead of a feverish, selfish little clot of ailments and grievances, complaining that the world will not devote itself to making you happy. I am of the opinion that my life belongs to the community, and as long as I live, it is my privilege to do for it what I can.

GEORGE BERNARD SHAW.

Only a life lived for others is a life worthwhile.

ALBERT EINSTEIN

● ● ●

The grand essentials of happiness are: something to do,
something to love, and something to hope for.
ALLAN K. CHALMERS

Founded on Faith

Creating a family in this turbulent world is an act of faith, a wager that against all odds there will be a future, that love can last, that the heart can triumph against all adversities and even against the grinding wheel of time.

DEAN KOONTZ

A mother's love is like a beacon
    Burning bright with Faith and Prayer
And through the changing scenes of life
    We can find a haven there....
For a mother's love is fashioned
    After God's enduring love,
It is endless and unfailing
    Like the love of Him above.

HELEN STEINER RICE

We ought always to give thanks to God for you,...as is only fitting, because your faith is greatly enlarged, and the love of each one of you toward one another grows ever greater.

2 THESSALONIANS 1:3 NASB

• • •

The first and finest lesson that parents can teach their children is faith and courage.
SMILEY BLANTON

Imagine All You Can

Imagination is the beginning of creation. You imagine what you desire, you will what you imagine and at last you create what you will.

GEORGE BERNARD SHAW

Look up to the skies.
Who created all these stars?
He leads out the army of heaven one by one
and calls all the stars by name.
Because He is strong and powerful,
not one of them is missing....
Surely you know. Surely you have heard.
The Lord is the God who lives forever,
who created all the world.
He does not become tired or need to rest.
No one can understand how great His wisdom is.
He gives strength to those who are tired
and more power to those who are weak.

ISAIAH 40: 26, 28-29 NCV

Reality can be beaten with enough imagination.

• • •

Every person's life is a fairy tale written by God's fingers.
HANS CHRISTIAN ANDERSEN

• • •

Childhood Memories

There was a place in childhood that I remember well,
And there a voice of sweetest tone bright fairy tales did tell.

SAMUEL LOVER

Memory is the treasury and guardian of all things.

CICERO

O Lord, You alone are my hope
I've trusted You, O Lord, from childhood.
Yes, You have been with me from birth;
from my mother's womb You have cared for me.
No wonder I am always praising You!
My life is an example to many,
because You have been my strength and protection.
That is why I can never stop praising You;
I declare Your glory all day long.

PSALM 71:5-8 NLT

Take the gift of this moment and make something beautiful of
it. Few worthwhile experiences just happen, memories are made
on purpose.

GLORIA GAITHER

• • •

How dear to the heart are the scenes of my childhood,
when fond recollection presents them to view.
SAMUEL WOODWORTH

Cultivate a Spirit of Joy

How necessary it is to cultivate a spirit of joy. It is a psychological truth that the physical acts of reverence and devotion make one feel devout. The courteous gesture increases one's respect for others. To act lovingly is to begin to feel loving, and certainly to act joyfully brings joy to others which in turn makes one feel joyful. I believe we are called to the duty of delight.

DOROTHY DAY

Serve each other with love. The whole law is made complete in this one command: "Love your neighbor as you love yourself."

GALATIANS 5:13-14 NCV

Joy is the feeling of grinning on the inside.

MELBA COLGROVE

• • •

Since you get more joy out of giving joy to others, you should put a good deal of thought into the happiness that you are able to give.
ELEANOR ROOSEVELT

● ● ●

Home of the Heart

My mother and I have laughed over nothing and cried over everything. We understand each other's fears, losses, and sense of humor. She holds my heart like no one else can.

Be devoted to one another in brotherly love. Honor one another above yourselves. Never be lacking in zeal, but keep your spiritual fervor, serving the Lord. Be joyful in hope, patient in affliction, faithful in prayer. Share with God's people who are in need. Practice hospitality.

ROMANS 12:10-13 NIV

No matter the distance between us, physical or emotional, there will always be one in the world who...knows the heart of me in a way that no other can. And should I ever know real trouble in my life, she will suddenly appear beside me, to hold my hand in hers.

ANTHONY BRANDT

• • •

*Our sweetest experiences of affection are meant to point us to
that realm which is the real and endless home of the heart.*
HENRY WARD BEECHER

Bloom Where You Are Planted

One of the most tragic things I know about human nature is
that all of us tend to put off living. We are all dreaming of
some magical rose garden over the horizon—instead of enjoying
the roses that are blooming outside our windows today.

DALE CARNEGIE

How strange is the lot of us mortals! Each of us is here for a
brief sojourn; for what purpose he knows not, though he senses
it. But without deeper reflection one knows from daily life that
one exists for other people.

ALBERT EINSTEIN

You wake up in the morning, and lo! your purse is magically
filled with twenty-four hours of the magic tissue of the universe
of your life. No one can take it from you. No one receives either
more or less than you receive. Waste your infinitely precious
commodity as much as you will, and the supply will never be
withheld from you. Moreover, you cannot draw on the future.
Impossible to get into debt. You can only waste the passing
movements. You cannot waste tomorrow. It is kept for you.

ARNOLD BENNETT

• • •

So then neither he who plants is anything, nor he who waters, but God who gives the increase. Now he who plants and he who waters are one, and each one will receive his own reward according to his own labor. For we are God's fellow workers.

1 CORINTHIANS 3:7-9 NKJV

Living Life

We live in the present, we dream of the future, but we learn eternal truths from the past. Isn't it splendid to think of all the things there are to find out about?

LUCY MAUD MONTGOMERY

You have begun to live the new life, in which you are being made new and are becoming like the One who made you. This new life brings you the true knowledge of God.

COLOSSIANS 3:10 NCV

Life is about not knowing, having to change, taking the moment and making the best of it, without knowing what's going to happen next. Delicious ambiguity.

GILDA RADNER

Here is the test to find whether your mission on Earth is finished: if you're alive, it isn't.
RICHARD BACH

At the Dinner Table

The most remarkable thing about my mother is that for thirty years she served the family nothing but leftovers. The original meal has never been found.

CALVIN TRILLIN

A mother is a person who, seeing there are only four pieces of pie for five people, promptly announces she never did care for pie.

TENNEVA JORDAN

Stay on good terms with each other, held together by love. Be ready with a meal or a bed when it's needed. Why, some have extended hospitality to angels without ever knowing it!

HEBREWS 13:1-2 THE MESSAGE

Man cannot live by bread alone; he needs peanut butter.

BARBARA JOHNSON

• • •

The incredible gift of the ordinary! Glory comes streaming from the table of daily life.
MACRINA WIEDERKEHR

● ● ●

Today and Always

Some say "tomorrow" never comes,
    A saying oft thought right;
But if tomorrow never came,
    No end were of "tonight."
The fact is this, time flies so fast,
    That e'er we've time to say
"Tomorrow's come," presto! behold!
    "Tomorrow" proves "Today."

Even though on the outside it often looks like things are falling
apart on us, on the inside, where God is making new life, not a
day goes by without His unfolding grace. These hard times are
small potatoes compared to the coming good times, the lavish
celebration prepared for us. There's far more here than meets the
eye. The things we see now are here today, gone tomorrow. But
the things we can't see now will last forever.

2 Corinthians 4:16-18 the message

Light tomorrow with today.

Elizabeth Barrett Browning

This day was yesterday tomorrow nam'd:
    Tomorrow shall be yesterday proclaimed:
Tomorrow not yet come, not far away,
    What shall tomorrow then be call'd? Today.

John Owen

• • •

*Live each day the fullest you can, not guaranteeing there'll be
a tomorrow, not dwelling endlessly on yesterday.*
JANE SEYMOUR

● ● ●

Learning About Life

God, help me to be honest so my children
   will learn honesty.
Help me to be kind so my children
   will learn kindness.
Help me to be faithful so my children
   will learn faith.
Help me to love so that my children
   will be loving.

MARIAN WRIGHT EDELMAN

Let me hear Your lovingkindness in the morning;
For I trust in You;
Teach me the way in which I should walk;
For to You I lift up my soul.

PSALM 143:8 NASB

You may have tangible wealth untold;
   Caskets of jewels and coffers of gold.
Richer than I you can never be—
   I had a mother who read to me.

STRICKLAND GILLILAN

• • •

The most important thing that parents can teach their children is how to get along without them.
FRANK A. CLARK

Beautiful Things

Christ's love makes the church whole. His words evoke her beauty. Everything He does and says is designed to bring the best out of her, dressing her in dazzling white silk, radiant with holiness.

Ephesians 5:25 the message

Real strength never impairs beauty or harmony, but it often bestows it; and in everything imposingly beautiful, strength has much to do with the magic.

Herman Melville

We are all cups, constantly and quietly being filled. The trick is, knowing how to tip ourselves over and let the beautiful stuff out.

Ray Bradbury

● ● ●

Though we travel the world over to find the beautiful,
we must carry it with us or we find it not.
RALPH WALDO EMERSON

The Ultimate Goal

Tell me not, in mournful numbers,
Life is but an empty dream!
For the soul is dead that slumbers,
and things are not what they seem.
Life is real! Life is earnest!
And the grave is not its goal;
Dust thou art; to dust returnest,
Was not spoken of the soul.

HENRY WADSWORTH LONGFELLOW

The goal of our instruction is love from a pure heart and a
good conscience and a sincere faith.

1 TIMOTHY 1:5 NASB

Dance like there's nobody watching
   Love like you'll never get hurt
Sing like there's nobody listening
   Live like it's heaven on earth
And speak from the heart to be heard.

WILLIAM W. PURKEY

● ● ●

The great use of life is to spend it for something that will outlast it.
WILLIAM JAMES

The Gift of Family

One of the greatest gifts
That life can give to anyone
Is the very special love that families share...
As years go by,
It's good to know that there will always be
Certain people in our lives who care.
For there are countless things
That only families have in common
And memories that no one else can make...
And these precious ties that bind a family together
Are bonds that time and distance cannot break.
How fortunate we are
When we have relatives to love us,
It makes the world a happy place to be....
Few gifts in life
Will last as long
Or touch the heart as deeply
As the very special gift
Of family.

CRAIG S. TUNKS

● ● ●

Let love and faithfulness never leave you;
bind them around your neck,
write them on the tablet of your heart.
PROVERBS 3:3 NIV

Let the Day Suffice

The simplest and commonest truth seems new and wonderful when we experience it the first time in our own life.

MARIE VON EBNER-ESCHENBACH

People who don't know God and the way He works fuss over these things, but you know both God and how He works. Steep your life in God-reality, God-initiative, God-provisions. Don't worry about missing out. You'll find all your everyday human concerns will be met.

MATTHEW 6:32-33 THE MESSAGE

Sooner or later we all discover that the important moments in life are not the advertised ones, not the birthdays, the graduations, the weddings, not the great goals achieved. The real milestones are less prepossessing. They come to the door of memory.

SUSAN B. ANTHONY

● ● ●

Let the day suffice, with all its joys and failings, its little triumphs and defeats. I'd happily, if sleepily, welcome evening as a time of rest, and let it slip away, losing nothing.
KATHLEEN NORRIS

Hugs and More Hugs

Mother love is the fuel that enables a normal human being to do the impossible.

MARION C. GARRETTY

You're blessed when you care. At the moment of being "care-full," you find yourselves cared for.

MATTHEW 5:7 THE MESSAGE

May you wake each day with God's blessings and sleep each night in His keeping. And as you grow older, may you always walk in His tender care.

I wish you love and strength and faith and wisdom,
Goods, gold enough to help some needy one.
I wish you songs, but also blessed silence,
And God's sweet peace when every day is done.

DOROTHY NELL MCDONALD

No one ever outgrows the need for a mother's love.
JANETTE OKE

● ● ●

Work-a-day World

Attempt easy tasks as if they were difficult, and difficult as if they were easy; in the one case that confidence may not fall asleep, in the other that it may not be dismayed.

BALTASAR GRACIAN

Don't just do what you have to do to get by, but work heartily, as Christ's servants doing what God wants you to do. And work with a smile on your face, always keeping in mind that no matter who happens to be giving the orders, you're really serving God. Good work will get you good pay from the Master.

EPHESIANS 6:6-8 THE MESSAGE

Respect human talent, respond to genius, recognize reality, admire truth and beauty, realize the meaning of the rare flower Reason.

PETER NIVIO ZARLENGA

Experience is that marvelous thing that enables you to recognize a mistake when you make it again.

FRANKLIN P. JONES

● ● ●

The secret of joy in work is contained in one word—excellence.
To know how to do something well is to enjoy it.
PEARL BUCK

Deep and Powerful Sense

For I am bound with fleshly bands,
    Joy, beauty, lie beyond my scope;
I strain my heart, I stretch my hands,
    And catch at hope.

CHRISTINA ROSSETTI

Hope is a state of mind, not of the world. Hope, in this deep
and powerful sense, is not the same as joy that things are going
well, or willingness to invest in enterprises that are obviously
heading for success, but rather an ability to work for something
because it is good.

VACLAV HAVEL

I pray also that the eyes of your heart may be enlightened in
order that you may know the hope to which He has called you,
the riches of His glorious inheritance in the saints, and His
incomparably great power for us who believe. That power is like
the working of His mighty strength.

EPHESIANS 1:18-19 NIV

• • •

Hope, like the gleaming taper's light,
Adorns and cheers our way;
And still, as darker grows the night,
Emits a brighter ray.
OLIVER GOLDSMITH

Show Me the Way to Go

In waiting we begin to get in touch with the rhythms of life.... They are the rhythms of God. It is in the everyday and the commonplace that we learn patience, acceptance, and contentment.

RICHARD J. FOSTER

Most important of all, continue to show deep love for each other.

1 PETER 4:8 NLT

What parent can tell when some fragmentary gift of knowledge or wisdom will enrich her children's lives? Or how a small seed of information passed from one generation to another may generate a new science, a new industry—a seed which neither the giver nor the receiver can truly evaluate at the time.

HELENA RUBINSTEIN

• • •

Tradition gives us a sense of solidarity and roots, a knowing there are some things one can count on.
GLORIA GAITHER

● ● ●

Dear God...

You are a child of your heavenly Father. Confide in Him. Your faith in His love and power can never be bold enough.

BASILEA SCHLINK

Where are you? Start there. Openly and freely declare your need to the One who cares deeply.

CHARLES R. SWINDOLL

We must take our troubles to the Lord, but we must do more than that; we must leave them there.

HANNAH WHITALL SMITH

Embrace this God-life. Really embrace it, and nothing will be too much for you.... That's why I urge you to pray for absolutely everything, ranging from small to large. Include everything as you embrace this God-life, and you'll get God's everything.

MARK 11:22-24 THE MESSAGE

● ● ●

You pay God a compliment by asking great things of Him.
TERESA OF AVILA

Roots and Wings

To be rooted is perhaps the most important and least recognized need of the human soul.

SIMONE WEIL

I rejoice in life for its own sake. Life is no "brief candle" to me. It is a sort of splendid torch which I have got hold of for the moment; and I want to make it burn as brightly as possible before handing it on to future generations.

GEORGE BERNARD SHAW

Don't let anyone look down on you because you are young, but set an example for the believers in speech, in life, in love, in faith and in purity.

1 TIMOTHY 4:12 NIV

• • •

*The greatest gifts you can give your children are the roots of
responsibility and the wings of independence.*
DENIS WAITLEY

● ● ●

Simple Things

I still find each day too short for all the thoughts I want to
think, all the walks I want to take, all the books I want to
read, and all the friends I want to see. The longer I live, the
more my mind dwells upon the beauty and the wonder of the
world.

JOHN BURROUGHS

God is the One who gives seed to the farmer and bread for food.
He will give you all the seed you need and make it grow so
there will be a great harvest from your goodness. He will make
you rich in every way so that you can always give freely. And
your giving through us will cause many to give thanks to God.
This service you do not only helps the needs of God's people, it
also brings many more thanks to God.

2 CORINTHIANS 9:10-12 NCV

Joys come from simple and natural things: mists over meadows,
sunlight on leaves, the path of the moon over water.

SIGURD F. OLSON

• • •

Grant me the power of saying things too simple and too sweet for words.
COVENTRY PATMORE

God Loves You

Just as there comes a warm sunbeam into every cottage window, so comes a love-beam of God's care for every separate need.

NATHANIEL HAWTHORNE

It is clear to us, friends, that God not only loves you very much but also has put His hand on you for something special.

1 THESSALONIANS 1:4 THE MESSAGE

Listening to God is a firsthand experience.... God invites you to vacation in His splendor. He invites you to feel the touch of His hand. He invited you to feast at His table. He wants to spend time with you.

MAX LUCADO

• • •

Open your hearts to the love God instills.... God loves you tenderly. What He gives you is not to be kept under lock and key, but to be shared.
MOTHER TERESA

Dress Up

Play is the business of childhood, and its continuation in later years is the prolongation of youth.

WALTER RAUSCHENBUSCH

Women know
    The way to rear up children (to be just);
They know a simple, merry, tender knack
    Of tying sashes, fitting baby-shoes,
And stringing pretty words that make no sense,
    And kissing full sense into empty words;
Which things are corals to cut life upon,
    Although such trifles.

ELIZABETH BARRETT BROWNING

Mingle a little folly with your wisdom; a little nonsense now and then is pleasant.

HORACE

Surprise us with love at daybreak;
then we'll skip and dance all the day long.

PSALM 90:14 THE MESSAGE

*Play allows us to be eternally young, to be like children
even when we are old and wrinkly.*
TERRY LINDVALL

Lovely Days

Our Creator would never have made such lovely days and given us the deep hearts to enjoy them, above and beyond all thought, unless we were meant to be immortal.

NATHANIEL HAWTHORNE

Whatever is true, whatever is noble, whatever is right, whatever is pure, whatever is lovely, whatever is admirable—if anything is excellent or praiseworthy—think about such things.

PHILIPPIANS 4:8 NIV

Instead of a gem, or even a flower, we should cast the gift of a lovely thought into the heart of a friend, that would be giving as the angels give.

GEORGE MACDONALD

*The uncertainties of the present always give way
to the enchanted possibilities of the future.*
GELSEY KIRKLAND

A Little Advice

Always stay connected to people and seek out things that bring you joy. Dream with abandon. Pray confidently.

BARBARA JOHNSON

My child, listen to your father's teaching and do not forget your mother's advice. Their teaching will be like flowers in your hair or a necklace around your neck.

PROVERBS 1:8 NCV

It is very difficult to live among people you love and hold back from offering them advice.

ANNE TYLER

May you live every day of your life.

JONATHAN SWIFT

• • •

Live your life while you have it. Life is a splendid gift—there is nothing small about it.
FLORENCE NIGHTINGALE

A Heart Full of Grace

Have you ever thought that in every action of grace in your heart
you have the whole omnipotence of God engaged to bless you?

ANDREW MURRAY

We throw open our doors to God and discover at the same
moment that He has already thrown open His door to us.
We find ourselves standing where we always hoped we might
stand—out in the wide open spaces of God's grace and glory,
standing tall and shouting our praise.

ROMANS 5:2 THE MESSAGE

Look deep within yourself and recognize what brings life and
grace into your heart. It is this that can be shared with those
around you. You are loved by God. This is an inspiration to love.

CHRISTOPHER DE VINCK

• • •

There is no rest in the heart of God until He knows that we are at rest in His grace.
LLOYD JOHN OGILVIE

The Gift of Miracles

Do not pray for easy lives. Pray to be stronger.... Do not pray for tasks equal to your powers. Pray for powers equal to your tasks. Then the doing of your work shall be no miracle, but you shall be the miracle.

PHILLIPS BROOKS

Because of His great love for us, God, who is rich in mercy, made us alive with Christ even when we were dead in transgressions.... And God raised us up with Christ and seated us with Him in the heavenly realms in Christ Jesus, in order that in the coming ages He might show the incomparable riches of His grace, expressed in His kindness to us in Christ Jesus.

EPHESIANS 2:4-7 NIV

There are only two ways to live your life. One is as though nothing is a miracle. The other is as though everything is a miracle.

RICHARD CRASHAW

• • •

*I think miracles exist in part as gifts and in part as clues
that there is something beyond the flat world we see.*
PEGGY NOONAN

• • •

Laughter and Tears

Sipping sodas during a movie
laughing loudly at something hilariously funny
eating pancakes quietly just us two
Girl time—our time
Holding each other and sobbing
hard
we made it through,
me and you...suffered it all
mother and daughter
friends till the end.

CATHERINE INSCORE

And now, God, do it again—
bring rains to our drought-stricken lives
So those who planted their crops in despair
will shout hurrahs at the harvest,
So those who went off with heavy hearts
will come home laughing, with armloads of blessing.

PSALM 126:3-5 THE MESSAGE

God makes our lives a medley of joy and tears, hope and help,
love and encouragement.

● ● ●

There isn't much that I can do,
but I can share my hopes with you,
and I can share my fears with you,
and sometimes shed some tears with you,
as on our way we go.

Our Hearts Entwined

May the Lord direct your hearts into the love of God and into the steadfastness of Christ.

2 Thessalonians 3:4-5 nasb

The fullness of our heart is expressed in our eyes, in our touch, in what we write, in what we say, in the way we walk, the way we receive, the way we need.

Mother Teresa

One of life's greatest treasures is the love that binds hearts together in friendship.

My purpose is that they may be encouraged in heart and united in love, so that they may have the full riches of complete under-standing, in order that they may know the mystery of God, namely, Christ, in whom are hidden all the treasures of wisdom and knowledge.

Colossians 2:2-3 niv

• • •

Only He who created the wonders of the world entwines hearts in an eternal way.

Legacies

Whenever I've needed someone to share my joy, or someone to hold me when my world rips to pieces, you're there. And I know you will be—tomorrow, always.

MAYA V. PATEL

Never forget that I love you more than any other person in the world, no matter how far apart we are you will always be my daughter.

There are only two lasting bequests we can hope to give our children. One of these is roots, the other, wings.

HODDING CARTER

I will make you beautiful forever, a joy to all generations.

ISAIAH 60:15 NLT

Tradition is a form of promise from parent to child. It's a way to say, "I love you," "I'm here for you," and "Some things will not change."
LYNN LUDWICK

• • •

The Secret of Abundant Life

Not what we have but what we enjoy constitutes our abundance.

JOHN PETIT-SENN

And this I pray, that your love may abound still more and more in real knowledge and all discernment, so that you may approve the things that are excellent, in order to be sincere and blameless until the day of Christ.

PHILIPPIANS 1:9-10 NASB

God made you so you could share in His creation, could love and laugh and know Him.

TED GRIFFEN

● ● ●

To love by freely giving is its own reward. To be possessed by love and to in turn give love away is to find the secret of abundant life.
GLORIA GAITHER

Kindred Spirits

The gift of friendship—both given and received—is joy, love and nurturing for the heart. The realization that you have met a soul mate...a kindred spirit...a true friend...is one of life's sweetest gifts!

Be of the same mind toward one another. Do not set your mind on high things, but associate with the humble.... If it is possible, as much as depends on you, live peaceably with all men.

ROMANS 12:16, 18 NKJV

Sometimes our light goes out but is blown into flame by another human being. Each of us owes deepest thanks to those who have rekindled this light.

ALBERT SCHWEITZER

And thou shalt in thy daughter see,
This picture, once, resembled thee.

AMBROSE PHILIPS

• • •

Anything, everything, little or big becomes an adventure when the right person shares it.
KATHLEEN NORRIS

God's Heart

The Lord your God is with you....
He will take great delight in you,
He will quiet you with His love,
He will rejoice over you with singing.

ZEPHANIAH 3:17 NIV

We think God's love rises and falls with our performance.
It doesn't.... He loves you for whose you are: you are
His child.

MAX LUCADO

There is no need to plead that the love of God shall fill our
hearts as though He were unwilling to fill us.... Love is
pressing around us on all sides like air. Cease to resist it
and instantly love takes possession.

AMY CARMICHAEL

● ● ●

God's heart is the most sensitive and tender of all. No act goes unnoticed, no matter how insignificant or small.
RICHARD FOSTER

Happiness Is...

An effort made for happiness of others lifts us above ourselves.

LYDIA MARIA CHILD

Your greatest pleasure is that which rebounds from hearts that you have made glad.

HENRY WARD BEECHER

Examine and see how good the Lord is. Happy is the person who trusts Him. You who belong to the Lord, fear Him! Those who fear Him will have everything they need.

PSALM 34:8-9 NCV

*Happiness comes of the capacity to feel deeply, to enjoy simply,
to think freely, to risk life, to be needed.*
STORM JAMESON

● ● ●

Heart to Heart Talks

In the end, those things that affect your life most deeply are too simple to talk about.

NELL BLAINE

Pleasant words are a honeycomb, sweet to the soul, and healing to the bones.

PROVERBS 16:24 NIV

A friend hears the song in my heart and sings it to me when my memory fails.

PIONEER GIRLS LEADERS' HANDBOOK

The heart hath its own memory,
like the mind,
And in it are enshrined
The precious keepsakes,
into which is wrought
The giver's loving thought.

LONGFELLOW

• • •

It is only with the heart that one can see rightly. What is essential is invisible to the eye.
ANTOINE DE SAINT-EXUPÉRY

● ● ●

Embraced by His Love

To be grateful is to recognize the love of God in everything
He has given us—and He has given us everything. Every
breath we draw is a gift of His love, every moment of
existence a gift of grace.

THOMAS MERTON

God wants to continually add to us, to develop and
enlarge us—always building on what He has already
taught and built in us.

A. B. SIMPSON

You're blessed when you're at the end of your rope. With less of
you there is more of God and His rule. You're blessed when
you feel you've lost what is most dear to you. Only then can
you be embraced by the One most dear to you.

MATTHEW 5:3-4 THE MESSAGE

● ● ●

*God in His ample love embraces our love with...a sort of tenderness,
and we must tread the Way to Him hand in hand.*
SHELDON VANAUKEN

A Gift from God

Life is so full of meaning and purpose, so full of beauty, beneath its covering, that you will find that earth but cloaks your heaven.

FRA GIOVANNI

Our God gives you everything you need, makes you everything you're to be.

2 THESSALONIANS 1:2 THE MESSAGE

God walks with us.... He scoops us up in His arms or simply sits with us in silent strength until we cannot avoid the awesome recognition that yes, even now, He is here.

GLORIA GAITHER

● ● ●

I asked God for all things that I might enjoy life.
He gave me life that I might enjoy all things.

Oh, To Be Content!

Contentment is a pearl of great price, and whoever procures it at the expense of ten thousand desires makes a wise and a happy purchase.

JOHN BALGUY

I have learned to be content whatever the circumstances. I know what it is to be in need, and I know what it is to have plenty. I have learned the secret of being content in any and every situation, whether well fed or hungry, whether living in plenty or in want. I can do everything through Him who gives me strength.

PHILIPPIANS 4:11-13 NIV

The secret of contentment is knowing how to enjoy what you have, and to be able to lose all desire for things beyond your reach.

LIN YU-T'ANG

● ● ●

*What makes us disconte n ted with our condition is the absurdly
exaggera ted idea we have of the happiness of others.*
FRENCH PROVERB

● ● ●

Tender Moments

Love grows from our capacity to give what is deepest within ourselves and also receive what is the deepest within another person. The heart becomes an ocean strong and deep, launching all on its tide.

Be kind to each other, tenderhearted, forgiving one another, just as God through Christ has forgiven you.

EPHESIANS 4:32 NLT

When the most important things in our life happen we quite often do not know, at the moment, what is going on.

C. S. LEWIS

● ● ●

If I could reach up and hold a star for every time you've made me smile,
the entire evening sky would be in the palm of my hand.

• • •

From His abundance we have all received
one gracious blessing after another.

JOHN 1:16 NLT